Initial Coin Offering

What You Need to Know to Pick a Profitable ICO

By

Jack Monroe

© **Copyright 2018 Jack Monroe**
All rights reserved.

The contents of this book may not be reproduced, duplicated or transmitted without direct written permission from the author. Under no circumstances will any legal responsibility or blame be held against the publisher for any reparation, damages, or monetary loss due to the information herein, either directly or indirectly.

Legal Notice

You cannot amend, distribute, sell, use, quote or paraphrase any part or the content within this book without the consent of the author.

Disclaimer Notice

Please note the information contained within this document is for educational and entertainment purposes only. No warranties of any kind are expressed or implied. Readers acknowledge that the author is not engaging in the rendering of legal, financial, medical or professional advice.

Please consult a licensed professional before attempting any techniques outlined in this book.

By reading this document, the reader agrees that under no circumstances are is the author responsible for any losses, direct or indirect, which are incurred as a result of the use of information contained within this document, including, but not limited to, —errors, omissions, or inaccuracies.

Jack Monroe

Contents

Introduction 7

Chapter 1: Initial Coin Offering Basics 9

Chapter 2: How ICOs Work 25

Chapter 3 - General Investing Guidelines 31

Chapter 4 - Storing Your Coins And Tokens 43

Chapter 5 - Investing In Cryptocurrencies 47

Chapter 6 - How To Avoid Being Scammed 69

Chapter 7 - How To Choose ICOs Wisely 83

Cryptocurrency Glossary 99

Conclusion 135

Jack Monroe

Introduction

Initial Coin Offerings, or ICOs are all the rage in the investment community these days. Why? It's because so many people have become millionaires practically overnight because of the phenomenal increases in market values of such assets. And you can become one too through ICO investing.

But there's more to it than meets the eye. In this book, you'll learn what ICOs are, their nuances, general investing principles and specific ICO and cryptocurrency investing principles to help you start investing in ICOs. I hope that, by the end of the book, you'll be able to make very informed decisions on whether to invest in ICOs or not and if you decide to do so, you'll be able to invest wisely.

So if you're ready, turn the page and let's begin!

Jack Monroe

Chapter 1: Initial Coin Offering Basics

From security to payments, to banking, blockchain technology has been changing the way things are done on a massive scale. But what's proving to be the most interesting part of this technology for established and startup companies is the way blockchain-based currencies, projects and the companies behind them raise funds, i.e., initial coin offerings. Also referred to as ICOs, this manner of raising funds is a very innovative and groundbreaking one that is changing timelines, boundaries and conventions changing how businesses are able to secure much needed financing in order to succeed.

ICOs seems to have burst out of the gates sometime in 2017 and has become Wall Street and Silicon Valley's newest obsession. Just to give you an idea of just how en vogue initial coin offerings are these days, crypto programmers were able to raise more than $4 billion in 2017 through ICOs, i.e., selling their own cryptocurrencies to investors who are looking for new ways to potentially earn huge returns on their monies.

So what are ICOs really? The simplest definition of it is that it's a financing activity that allows online projects and start-up companies to raise the necessary funds and the need to go to venture capitalists or sell shares of stock of their company. It's akin to IPOs - or initial public offerings - of stocks and bonds hence the similarity in terminologies and acronyms. And it's not just start-ups and online projects that can use this groundbreaking financing approach. Established manufacturing businesses can also raise money using this financing model.

As mentioned earlier, crypto programmers solicit funds by coming up with their own crypto or virtual currencies and selling them to the investing public. These newly created currencies follow similar guidelines and rules as those of established cryptocurrencies such as Bitcoin and Ethereum (Ether). ICOs also accept payments for their newly created coins in the form of other established ones like, again, Bitcoin and Ether. The newly issued coins or tokens underlying ICOs are often structured in ways that they can only be used on the computing platform that the ICOs crypto programmers are trying to create.

Compared to traditional IPOs that are very standardized and require a lot of legal work, ICOs are way different. For example, investors pay for newly issued shares of stocks of a company using fiat currency or money in initial public offerings. And these shares of stocks, or equities as they're commonly referred to, provide investors with some level of control or say in the company via voting rights. And, in countries like the United States, investment banks perform or are responsible for carrying out companies' IPOs and the Federal government via the Securities and Exchange Commission or SEC regulates such activities very closely.

When it comes to ICOs, no such things are needed. There's no need for an investment bank to manage the fund raising activity, shares of stock and voting rights are rarely given to investors, and there's hardly any government oversight involved. The latter, however, may soon change because of a new task force that the United States' SEC has created. Also, projects or start-ups that do ICOs hardly have any corporate track record or finished product in the market.

People who are in favor of ICOs make the case for it by pointing out to how the venture capital process is sped up and becomes more democratic by ICOs. Those who aren't as convinced by ICOs on the other hand, argue that the way ICOs operate is nothing short of ludicrous. Whether ICOs are an ingenious way of raising funds and generating handsome investment returns for investors or a total scam is determined by which side of the ICO fence you stand. But regardless of which side you're standing, there's no doubt that ICOs aren't something to take lightly. Remember, that ICOs were able to raise more than $4 billion for their projects proponents in 2017 alone.

One of the biggest - if not the biggest - ICO in the history of, well, ICOs is Filecoin, which was able to raise more than $250 million in funding for a mega global cloud storage project that it planned to build using the money raised. Another thing that went in favor of Filecoin was the fact that it was the very first ICO that was considered to be SEC-compliant.

With ICOs, one of the most prominent operative terms most frequently used is "promising to build." This is because as mentioned earlier, ICOs hardly have any corporate track record or existing product to speak of, and the fundraising activities are meant to fund startup projects or companies. This means ICOs are very high risk investments, which also means the opportunities to earn huge returns are off the charts.

In that case, you may be wondering: "What'll happen to my money if the projects' proponents don't follow through with their promises or plans?" Well, you lose all your money if that happens. Investors really don't have any resort when this happens because by nature, ICOs are practically unregulated and projects like Filecoin chose to comply with the SEC's new rules. Most ICOs choose not to because they feel it may impair their ability to successfully raise the funds that they need. That's why investing in ICOs is a high stakes game that requires a lot of very good research and investment savvy to successfully pull off.

Why Skip The Venture Capitalists?

At this point, I think it's clear that crypto programmers who want to maximize the amount of money that they can raise for their projects believe that ICOs are the better option compared to traditional venture capitalist ones. If you want to understand why they believe so, consider two cryptocurrency companies Coinbase and Filecoin. Coinbase was only able to raise $100 million after five years from it being founded via traditional venture capitalism. Filecoin on the other hand was able to raise over $250 million through an ICO despite not having any working product yet. Go figure.

And here's an even more compelling reason for startups choosing to go down the ICO route instead of turning to venture capitalists: control retention. As I explained earlier, ICOs normally don't give shares of stock and consequently, voting rights, to investors. Conversely, angel investors or venture capitalists normally aren't comfortable with having no say or control over the activities of the company they helped fund to life. And more importantly, ICO proponents get to keep their proprietary technologies proprietary.

Lastly, programmers also resort to ICOs simply because some projects are off limits for most venture capitalists. Why? Many ICO projects are by nature, open-sourced. What this means is that by the time a project is completed, it's owned by no one in particular and owned by everybody similar to how Ether and Bitcoin are because of underlying blockchain technology. No venture capitalist in their right frame of mind would fund something that they don't get to own whether in whole or in part. Take for example Filecoin. It's cloud storage network project will ultimately be operated by its users and not by its investors or programmers.

If That's The Case, Why Do People Invest In ICOs?

Believe it or not, people have a basis for investing in ICOs despite the seemingly high risk. They're banking on the services for which the tokens from ICOs will be used. However, none of the projects funded by ICOs have been completed as of the moment. So why do people still snap up ICOs like they were a newly opened bag of Lays chips?

Well, it's because even though the projects for which earlier ICOs were conducted are still being completed, investors are hoping that by the time the projects are finished, the value of the coins that will be used to transact for the projects will be much, much higher than the one at which they were sold during the ICOs. And even if the projects are still being completed, investors strongly believe that the prices of tokens launched via ICOs will continue going up as the projects near completion.

Take for example the Stratis token that was released in 2016. At the time of release, its price was only 7/10 of a penny, or $0.007. By the end of April 2018, its price was at $6.91 for a price multiple of 987 times or a 98,714% rate of return in just 2 years! That's how bullish the market for ICOs is at the moment.

Do you still wonder why people want to buy tokens via ICOs? High risk, high potential returns.

The ICO-Existing Cryptocurrencies Connection

Tokens or coins issued via ICOs are usually motivated by more established ones like Bitcoin and Ether in the sense that they also feature a cap or limit on the number of units that can ever be created or minted in order to create a sense of scarcity similar to that of precious metals like gold and silver. And like the two cryptocurrency pioneers, ICO tokens or coins are also structured in ways that make them decentralized and autonomous from any government financial regulators.

Another way by which new tokens issued via ICOs are related to existing ones is payments. In particular, ICOs primarily raise cryptocurrency funds instead of fiat ones. And more than just having cryptocurrency-based payments or funds, many of the tokens from ICOs are kept and transferred around using other variants of the Ethereum blockchain technology. But despite these relationships, ICO tokens or coins are still different from and independent of Bitcoin, Ethereum, and other alt coins.

Autonomous But Legal?

While ICOs naturally take on the decentralized and autonomous nature of their underlying cryptocurrencies and blockchain technologies, their legal statuses are somewhat vague in most countries, save for China and South Korea who have already decreed that ICOs are illegal. In the United States, the Securities and Exchange Commission or SEC maintains that some coins need to be classified as securities akin to how bonds and stocks are treated. As such, they need to be registered with the SEC before being offered to the general investing public. So in the United States, ICOs are legal but need to comply with their new regulations that govern the activity. So far, ICOs such as Filecoin's and Coinlist's complied with the new SEC regulations for initial coin offerings and their massive successes may inspire others to follow suit.

General Investor Sentiment

Several investors who are prominent in Silicon Valley strongly believe that ICOs can help create a way for open-source projects that would've been hard-pressed to get traditional funding to be completed successfully. Some of them even believe that ICOs may help pave the way for breakthrough open-source protocols for the Internet, which can eventually loosen the grip of online giants like Facebook and Google over the web.

One of the partners of a prominent American venture capitalist firm Andreessen Horowitz - Chris Dixon - believes that developing new open networks via ICOs can help make the Internet undo the Internet's centralized nature. And when that happens, he believes that the Internet will not just stay accessible, fair and vibrant but can help facilitate even more innovation.

But of course, there will always be skeptics - and that's a good thing. They bring the necessary checks and balance to a relatively unregulated industry. Such people think that most of the ICO projects won't succeed and will eventually lose money for their investors. They even think that because of such high risks, ICOs shouldn't even be happening at all.

Potential Returns On Investments

The high-risk nature of cryptocurrencies and consequently ICOs means that there is a lot of profit that can be made with ICOs. In fact, many ICO investors have already enjoyed huge profits because they were able to jump on the bandwagon at the lowest possible price point. The prices at which most - if not all - coins and tokens were sold during ICOs is considered by many as the lowest potential price points because of the way prices soared (literally) after the ICOs. These returns are often measured in what's called as price-gains multipliers, which is computed by dividing the difference between the current market price and the ICO price by the ICO price. A multiple of 1x (read as one time) means that the price increase of an asset is the same amount as the price at which it was bought and a multiple of 2x (two times) means the profit or gain is double the amount paid for the asset. It's not far-fetched to expect a minimum price-gains multiple of 10x for most ICOs. If you don't believe me, check out the top 10 ICOs in terms of price-gains multiples as of 3 May 2018 courtesy of https://icostats.com/roi-since-ico

Rank	COIN	Price Change Since ICO	Price-Gains Multiple
1	NXT	1,226,037%	12,260.37 X
2	IOTA	461,002%	4,610.02 X
3	NEO	237,782%	2,377.82 X
4	ETHER	207,967%	2,079.67 X
5	STRATIS	84,022%	840.22 X
6	SPECTRECOIN	83,518%	835.18 X
7	ARK	34,555%	345.55 X
8	LISK	14,955%	149.55 X
9	STORJ	9,540%	95.40 X
10	POPULOUS	8,216%	82.16 X

Based on this table, can you see how millionaires are made through cryptocurrencies, particularly through ICOs? Let's take a look at the lowest - Populous, the ICO of which was in June 2017. If you invested around $12,200 last year in this ICO when it was offered at $0.28 per unit, you'd have 1,000,000 dollars by 3 May 2018!

Jack Monroe

Chapter 2: How ICOs Work

Normally, an ICO starts by issuing a statement, which is usually in the form of what's called a "white paper," which provides detailed information about a project's plans, technical details, budget, goals, and how the tokens will be distributed, similar to prospectuses of initial public offerings. It's worth noting that what distinguishes coins from tokens is that the former represents currency ownership while the latter represents a stake in the autonomous organization or project.

Consistent with cryptocurrencies and the blockchain technology on which ICOs are built on, ICOs normally set a fixed number of coins or tokens that will ever be released or minted prior to the sale. At times, the earliest investors of ICOs are given incentives such as the option to buy coins or tokens at a lower price. But given the volatility of market prices of coins and tokens, the very high possibility that a lot of investors would want to participate, and the limited supply of tokens and coins, ICO investors will most probably get fewer units than what they initially signed up for.

Some ICOs have a specific number in mind when it comes to the amount of funds to be raised and as such, may opt to peg the price of the coins or tokens offered all throughout the ICO period. Some ICOs may choose to adjust the price according to demand for the tokens or coins and are open to raising as many funds possible.

Most ICOs in the past have been conducted indecently, which means they've been managed solely by the fundraising entity via its own platform or site. But as the demand for more security has increased, the more credible ICOs are now doing it with the help of an escrow service or an established exchange in order to provide prospective investors some sense of security that theirs aren't scams.

Despite incidences of ICO scams and poor-quality coins and tokens that have seemed to increase public distrust in ICOs and cryptocurrencies in general, many companies and startups remain unfazed and unwavering in their plans to raise funds through ICOs.

The Ideal ICO Platform

The social network called Kik was able to generate close to $100 million in funding in September 2017 through its initial coin offering. And their platform of choice? Ethereum. And Kodak - yes, that supposedly extinct technology company - proclaimed in January 2018 that they'd be launching their own cryptocurrency and blockchain service that aims to help photographers monetize their photos and shield them from unlicensed uses of such. As a result of said announcement, its stock price soared to more than double. Kodak is a very good example of how old-school companies can utilize the blockchain and cryptography technology via ICOs to not just survive but to thrive!

Both Kik and Kodak's ICOs were purposefully based on the Ethereum platform. One of the reasons for it is that more than just being a tradable cryptocurrency, the Ethereum platform enables programmers to create their own tokens and coins easily and launch their own ICOs. And even better, more and more of the world's biggest companies and learning institutions are embracing this platform.

But what really sets it apart as an ideal platform on which to launch an ICO are its extensible blockchain and smart contracts feature. In particular, the smart contract feature ensures that both parties to a contract fulfill their end of the bargain prior to settlement or complete execution. This helps provide users of a particular cryptocurrency or blockchain higher security compared to other blockchain platforms.

But while Ethereum seems to be the ideal platform for many ICOs, it doesn't mean it's perfect. For example, the Decentralized Autonomous Organization - better known as DAO - was able to generate up to $150 million worth of Ethereum coin funding, which is considered to be an international crowdfunding record. But almost immediately, more than $50 million worth of Ether coins raised through the funding were stolen or hacked. The administrators of the Ethereum platform were able to help DAO recover part of the stolen coins, but the fact remains that DAO lost a substantial amount of funds because of system imperfections. This story is one of the reasons why ICO investing isn't for the faint of heart.

But after that incident, it seems that the Ethereum platform's administrators doubled down on tightening the platform's security because subsequently, many ICOs were successful - and securely - launched on the platform. These ICOs include Iconomi, Augur, and Golem. And the platform seems to be gaining even more momentum now based on an analysis conducted by a leading site called TechCrunch. It notes that most of the 2017-launched ICOs were launched on the platform. Further, TechCrunch said that 2/3 of all cryptocurrencies as of July 2017 were Ethereum-based. In the next chapters, we'll take a more detailed look at investing in initial coin offerings or ICOs. We'll start with general investing guidelines (take note, guidelines and not rules) and towards the end of the book, we'll narrow it down to ICOs in particular.

Chapter 3 - General Investing Guidelines

While this book specifically covers ICO investing, it's best to start with general investing principles or guidelines because seeing the bigger picture will help you better grasp the smaller picture, i.e., the ICO sub-niche. And we'll begin with your reasons for investing money.

So Tell Me Why

Investing - especially investing in ICOs for the first time - has the potential to affect your life. As such, one of the most important things to do before pushing through with your ICO investing plans is this: Why am I doing this? This question may seem a bit irrelevant to investing and more relevant to spiritual and general life improvement matters but believe me, it is relevant to investing. And here's why.

There's a religious saying that before people build a house, one should first count the cost. I believe it's not just applicable to building houses but to any serious life endeavors, e.g., getting married, getting married, getting married, and investing. Pardon the emphasis on marriage, but ask married people and you'll get what I mean. Anyway, going back to counting the cost, everything has a cost whether it's getting married (there I go again), traveling around the world, or doing missionary work in a 5th world country (my terminology for countries that are really dirt poor). Investing is no different as it'll cost you money, time, and some sleepless nights to make more money.

Now how is your investing "why" related to the cost? Well, having a genuinely compelling reason will help you determine whether the cost is worth it. And if you do decide that the potential costs are worth it, having a very compelling reason for investing your money will help you stay the course when your investments aren't panning out as well as you'd like them to.

Take for example domestic helpers from third world countries like the Philippines. Many Filipina families live in poverty in that part of Southeast Asia and worse, there's not a lot of good-enough paying jobs available in the country for the parents of these families. As such, the mothers are often forced to look for jobs abroad as domestic helpers or maids.

Now I'm telling you, being a maid in a rich foreign country whose citizens feel so entitled that they think paying another human being to serve them as maids include the right to torture them physically and emotionally isn't easy at all. These Filipina women not only have to endure the deep sadness and loneliness of being away from their families for years on end but also the cruelty of many rich masters whose brains seem to be poorer than the poorest third world country. But even when war breaks out in the countries where they work or when their President imposes a total deployment ban to such countries, they'd willingly stay and endure the hardships.

Why? Because they have a very compelling reason, and that is their family's economic survival. If they come home because of their personal hardships at work, they won't be able to find jobs that will pay at least the same as their jobs abroad. For them, seeing their families' needs unmet is greater torture than being safe and at home with them. And this is one of the many compelling reasons that enable Filipina domestic helpers bear great hardships away from their families and persevere in working for very abusive masters.

Now I'm not saying investing in general and in ICOs, in particular, can be akin to being away from your friends and family while working for a very abusive master. But what I'm saying is there will be times when your self-control and willpower will be tested. Especially with high-risk and relatively volatile investments such as cryptocurrencies, there may be times when you'll have to bear relatively high financial and emotional costs, i.e., losses and anxiety, respectively. Without a compelling reason, it can be very tempting to quit early in the game or not even get into it at all.

So what are compelling investment reasons? Let me answer them by giving you examples of flimsy ones first:
- I just want to make more money;
- I want to be able to buy anything I want anytime I want; and
- I want to buy a Bugatti sports car.

To know your compelling reason, ask yourself the reasons for your relatively flimsy reasons. For example, why do you want to make more money? What do you need more money for? Why do you want to be able to buy anything you want? Is it because it makes you feel like a whole person? Or do you just want bragging rights? Examples of compelling reasons include:

- I want my child to be the first in our clan to get a college degree;
- I want to make sure that I can leave my children a very substantial inheritance when I die; and
- I want to make sure that I can retire early and focus on doing things that matter most to me like spending more time with my spouse and doing charity work in very poor places around the world.

Another benefit of having a clear and compelling investment reason is the ability to determine your minimum required rate of return on your investments. For example, having your child's college education as your compelling reason will lead you to study how much that would cost by the time he or she graduates from high school. Using the principle of time value of money, you can reasonably estimate how much money you'll need to invest, when to invest them, and more importantly, the minimum rate of return needed for you to be able to successfully fund your child's college education.

Minimum Rate Of Return

When you're lined up in a buffet that features practically all types of international and local cuisine, choosing which and how much to eat can be very stressful. Why? One of the reasons is because everything looks so delicious and you'll probably feel like you want to eat all of them, which may prove to be impossible. In other words, having no objective basis for choosing which foods to eat and how much of them to eat make deciding with certainty and finality very challenging.

Fortunately for investing, there's a highly - not perfectly - objective way of being able to choose your investments wisely, whether it's between different financial assets or within a specific genre of financial assets. And that is using expected rates of return.

But here's the thing about rates of return, if you want more of it, you'll have to be comfortable taking much higher financial risks. You see, the relationship between risk and return is one that's stronger than most friendships, families, and marriages. In case you're not familiar with the risk-return principle, it says that the higher your expected returns, the higher your risks are. It's that simple. The reason why the interest rates on bank deposits or the rates of return on treasury bills are very low is because their risks are very low too. On the other hand, the reason why it's not unheard of for ICOs to generate insanely high price-gains multipliers is because of their inherently uber-risky nature. Remember how we discussed in the previous chapter about how ICOs practically have very little - if any - to show for the tokens or coins being offered to the general public because most of them are startups? That makes them a very risky investment that's not for the faint of heart and the shallow of wallets.

When it comes to taking on risky investments, there are two important things you'll need to consider: your risk appetite and risk tolerance. Risk appetite is the mental aspect of risk. How much risk are you comfortable taking and by comfortable, I mean how you feel about the amount of risk. Take for example introducing yourself to a very attractive stranger from across the bar. The risk of being rejected or turned away is 50% and the impact of that risk happening is negligible, except probably for the ego. Objectively speaking, there's no harm in trying and failing. But it's a different thing when talking about how you feel about that risk. For many people, they're more afraid of being rejected by a very attractive stranger than bungee jumping, which can lead to death if things go wrong. For such people, their risk tolerance for introducing themselves to a beautiful stranger is much lower than their risk tolerance for jumping off a very high platform with nothing but rubber bands strapped to their feet and legs.

Risk tolerance, on the other hand, has less to do about how you feel but how much you can actually take regardless of how confident you feel about taking them. What do I mean by this? It means it's possible that you are comfortable taking financial risks on certain investments but you may not be able to recover financially if and when things go south. Allow me to illustrate.

There was a financial scam in Southeast Asia several years ago and one of the stories that really crushed my heart was that of a retired school principal's. He invested his all his retirement money in the investment scam, having been promised it will double in amount in just a few short months. Considering he's already retired, you can tell that his financial risk tolerance was already very low and he shouldn't have taken that risk. But because he didn't know better, he inadvertently took on a risk that was way beyond what his personal finances at his age can tolerate. He committed suicide after that.

When talking about risk tolerance, there are several factors to consider. One is age. Generally speaking, the older you are, the less financial risk you can tolerate. This is because the older you are, the less time and opportunities you have for recovering financially. That's why people who are in their 20s can afford to invest a much larger portion of their investible money in higher risk assets and people in their late 50s shouldn't be investing so much of their investible money in very high risk financial assets.

Another factor to consider is the financial position. People like Warren Buffet, despite his old age, can afford to invest tens of millions of dollars in cryptocurrencies or ICOs because compared to his overall financial position, ten, twenty, or even thirty million dollars is just a drop in the bucket. If he loses, it won't affect seriously his overall financial position. A stronger financial position will allow you to take on higher financial risk and potentially earn so much more.

Jack Monroe

Chapter 4 - Storing Your Coins And Tokens

Investing in ICOs mean you'll be investing in digital assets, i.e., cryptocurrencies. Being digital in form and without any physical counterpart, it's very important for you to be able to store your tokens and coins safely and securely, regardless if they're from ICOs or from already existing ones. And for this, you'll need a wallet.

A cryptocurrency wallet is a means by which to store your cryptocurrencies, much like your regular wallet that you use to store your paper bills and coins. Wallets can be classified into hot and cold storage wallets. Hot storage wallets are online wallets, i.e., wallets that you maintain either on the ICO platform or on a cryptocurrency exchange. Cold storage wallets are offline wallets, which are either in the form of an app that's installed on a computer or electronic device that's hardly ever online except for when transacting cryptocurrencies (software wallet), or a USB-type device dedicated for cryptocurrency storage only (hardware wallet).

Which type of wallet is best for storing your coins or tokens? Hardware cold storage wallets are. The primary reason is because it's an offline type of wallet. Because of their digital nature, coins and tokens can be easily stolen via hacking. So the best security measure for your coins and tokens is to store them offline because no Internet, no hack.

Another reason why hardware storage wallets are preferred over software wallets is because they have lower risks for losing your coins or tokens. If the computer or gadget on which your software app's installed, your wallet can be permanently corrupted or lost if the device or gadget becomes severely or terminally damaged. Worse, it can be hacked if you have the computer or device repaired by a devious repairman who knows a thing or two about cryptocurrency investing. With a hardware cold storage wallet, that won't happen because it's a stand-alone wallet, i.e., it's independent of your computer or gadget. The only way you can lose the coins or tokens stored in such a wallet is if you lose it or if you physically damage it.

Which brand of hardware wallets should you get? The most recommended among serious cryptocurrency investors are Nano Ledger S, Trezor, and KeepKey. They may cost a bit of money, but for the peace of mind they can give you, I'd say they're well worth it.

Jack Monroe

Chapter 5 - Investing In Cryptocurrencies

Now that you're familiar with general investment principles, it's time to narrow down our focus on investing in cryptocurrencies, i.e., coins and tokens. And in the final chapter, we'll focus on ICOs in particular.

Cryptocurrencies are a relatively young and risky class of financial assets for several reasons we covered earlier such as being a purely digital asset and its prices are highly dependent on investors' perceptions or market psychology, i.e., highly subjective, which makes it a relatively volatile financial asset. But as you've learned also, there can be no great rewards without great risks so at some point, you will need to take higher financial risks to optimize your chances of successfully meeting your investment goals. Here are some very important things to consider when investing in cryptocurrencies.

Do The Math

Investing is a numbers game, and by that, I don't mean by volume. The amount you'll invest, the rates of return you'll require, estimated or expected returns on financial assets - all of those are numbers. So if you hate numbers and you want to succeed at investing in cryptocurrencies, then you're going to have problems.

Fortunately, the math required to invest successfully isn't rocket science and there are easy-to-access tools like Microsoft Excel or Apple's Numbers to help you perform the important mathematical functions. And some of the most important mathematical concepts you'll need to familiarize yourself with are the mean or average, volatility or standard deviation, and time value of money.

The mean or average as applied to returns can give you reasonable expectations about future returns based on historical price performance. The standard deviation can give you reasonable expectations regarding the range of possible range of values for returns on a cryptocurrency in the future, i.e., a minimum and maximum expected rate of return or loss. And time value of money can help you determine how much money you'll need to invest now (present value) to get a specific amount in the future (future value), how much you'll get in the future if you invest a sum of money now, and the minimum required rate of return on your investments that will allow you to determine which among your cryptocurrency alternatives can help you achieve your investment goals best.

Research

Success favors the prepared, so they say. And when it comes to optimizing your chances of achieving your investment goals, nothing is as important as good research. There's a saying that "...people perish for lack of knowledge." and that's very much applicable to investors. The retired school principal lost practically everything because he didn't know enough about investments and how legit ones really work. So doing good research won't just lower your risks for loss, but can increase your chances of investment success.

So what are the things you'll need to research on regarding cryptocurrencies? If you're considering buying coins and tokens after an ICO, i.e., in the secondary market, historical prices are important. That's the only way you can objectively determine their historical price performance, which will be your primary basis for estimating their expected future rates of return - or loss. Another thing you must research about for cryptocurrencies in general, whether coins and tokens of an ongoing ICO or from the secondary market, is business and regulatory developments. Changes in technology, business practices, and financial regulatory framework can affect the potential price movements of cryptocurrencies primarily by affecting investors' general expectations of them. If you're up-to-date or aware of recent and ongoing developments in the world of business, technology, and regulatory environment, you'll be able to much better understand how investors may or may not feel towards cryptocurrencies in general and ICOs in particular. And when you're able to do that, your chances of being able to successfully choose winning cryptocurrencies will be much higher. Remember, the values of cryptocurrencies are primarily dependent on the market's sentiment towards them so by knowing how the market thinks can go a long way towards achieving your investment goals through coins and tokens.

Diversification

I'm sure you've heard or read about not putting all your eggs in one basket. There's a good reason for that. If that basket breaks or comes crashing down, all your eggs are cracked! But if you distribute them across two or three baskets, the crash of one will only affect some of your eggs, not all.

You can think of your cryptocurrency investments as your baskets where you put your money "eggs." Think about this: cryptocurrencies, especially ICOs, are inherently delicate baskets, i.e., very high risk. Can you imagine the risk you'll put your eggs in if you put all of them in just one very delicate basket? So even if you've diversified your investible funds among several asset classes like stocks, bonds, and cryptocurrencies, it's still a very good idea to diversify your cryptocurrency investments among two or three variants. That way, you can reduce your investment risks even further. That way, if one ICO or cryptocurrency investment doesn't pan out the way you want it to, possible losses can be limited to just that one investment and your other ICO or cryptocurrency investments won't be negatively affected.

Cost Averaging

Cost averaging is a strategy that can help you turn a seemingly losing cryptocurrency investment a profitable one or substantially reduce the losses incurred. Cost averaging is one of the oldest investment strategies in the book where you buy more units of a specific financial asset when its price goes down. At first glance, this seems counterproductive or downright illogical because why would you buy more units of an asset whose price has already gone down?

Here's the logic behind it: by buying more units at a much lower price, you bring down your average purchase cost per unit of a financial asset. With a lower average purchase cost per unit, your breakeven price becomes lower too, which means greater chances of not just breaking even but also earning more. Allow me to illustrate with an example.

Let's say you bought two units of Ethereum for $700 each, which is your initial average purchase cost. Your total cost is $1,400 for the two units. If the price of Ether goes down to only $500 per unit, your paper loss would be $200 per unit or $400 total. For you to recover the $400 total loss, you'll have to wait for the price of Ether to fully recover back to $700 per unit and for you to make money, you'd have to wait for it to go higher than that.

If you bought three more unit of Ether at the lower price of $500, your total investment would increase to $1,900 for the three units, at which point your average purchase cost per unit would drop to only $633.33 per unit ($1,900 ÷ 3 Ether units). This means you breakeven price went down to only $633.33 instead of the original $700 and by the time its price goes back up to $700, you could already cash in and make a profit of $66.67 ($700 - $633.33) per unit or a total of $200.01.

Now you see the power of cost averaging?

But what if the price goes down further? Well, unless there are indications that the cryptocurrency you're holding's doomed, you can buy more units. That's because there's a pretty good chance its price can recover.

You can use the cost averaging strategy on both existing and ICO coins or tokens. For ICOs, you can simply buy more of them in the secondary market once they're launched publicly.

Trading Or Investing

There are two general approaches to investing in coins and tokens: short-term or long-term. Short-term investing is more commonly known as "trading," i.e., buying and selling cryptocurrencies at a relatively fast clip. When trading, you can buy a coin or token now then sell it within the day, week, or month at a substantial profit and buying it again to do the same once prices dip substantially. Trading is the best way to optimize your investment returns for cryptocurrencies that have somewhat plateaued and whose prices seem to move predictively well within a general price range, i.e., high and low prices.

Long-term investing, also referred to as HODLing or a buy-and-hold approach, is a passive investment strategy, i.e., one that doesn't need a lot of monitoring or management. This is ideal for more established cryptocurrencies who already have a track record of success and solid indicators of potential long-term growth or development. It's challenging to use the buy-and-hold approach to ICOs because again, their lack of track record or actual product upon which to base future expectations of price. For ICOs, a more appropriate strategy - especially for people who don't have a lot of financial leeway - is the trading one. But if your risk tolerance and appetite are high, a long-term approach or HODLing can work well for ICOs too because you won't be greatly affected by wild price swings or losses due to the programmers' inability to follow through on what they promised to build.

If you choose to go down the trading route, keep in mind a couple of very important things. One of them is you'll need to constantly monitor the prices of your cryptocurrencies. By doing so, you can optimize your chances of being able to successfully execute profitable trades. And this means you'll need to dedicate a good chunk of time to doing this. If you're the type who has a day job that requires much focus, trading may not be a good route for you to take when investing in cryptocurrencies.

Another thing you'll need to keep in mind if you're considering going down the trading route is experience and feel of the market. Unless you have enough experience and ability to anticipate how cryptocurrency markets behave, all the time in the world may not help you execute enough successful trades. How you time your buy and sell transactions will determine whether your trades will be generally successful and that ability is dependent on how well you know the specific market for specific cryptocurrencies. And market knowledge and experience takes time. In most cases, traders start as long-term investors and as they accumulate market knowledge and experience, they're able to shift to trading.

Lastly, you'll need to keep in mind that successful trading isn't equal to perfect trading. What this means is it's alright if you execute losing trades every now and then. What's important is that as a whole, your trades are successful. By this I mean you have a positive bottom line for a specific period. For example, most of your trades for the week may be losing ones, but if you had a few trades that were big enough to give you a nice profit at the end of the week, that's successful trading. It's all about the bottom line. Consequently, it doesn't matter if 90% of your trades were profitable if the remaining 10%'s losses were so big that your overall trading performance results in a loss.

If you go down the route of long-term investing, most of the work you'll have to put in will be for research. You want to have a solid basis for committing to a specific ICO or cryptocurrency for the long haul and not just because the markets are feeling good about the future, especially for ICOs that generally have no track records or actual products to speak of while they're being done. You need to be able to dig deep and see whether or not the business model and the technology upon which the project that will be funded by the ICO has a high probability of growth and success. If you're in it for the long haul, it's better to err on the side of caution: if you don't find enough compelling information that will support the belief that it has a very good chance of success, stay off that particular ICO or already-existing token or coin.

How Much To Invest?

To answer this question, we'll have to go back to our discussion on risk tolerance. Remember we talked about basing it on your age and financial position? For the amount, I'll focus on financial position because this is the main determinant of how much you should invest.

The first question you must answer is how much investible funds do you have? By investible, I mean an amount that you can consider as excess funds after taking into consideration your buffer or emergency fund (about three to six months' worth of expenses) and money set aside for important use within the year.

The second question to ask yourself is out of the total investible funds, how much of it can you consider as dispensable, i.e., you're comfortable losing? Your answer to this question is the maximum amount you should invest in riskier assets like stocks and cryptocurrencies. A related question you can also ask yourself is out of the total investible funds, how much of those funds do you think will be needed within the next twelve to twenty-four months? This is a good estimate of the amount of funds you can invest because if you generally expect not to need such an amount in the next two years, then you won't be under much pressure when prices fluctuate downward in between.

Choose Your Crypto

This is where the rubber meets the coin - or the token. What should be your criteria for choosing which cryptocurrencies to invest in. There are research approaches you can use: quantitative and qualitative. The quantitative approach is more suited for cryptocurrencies that already have a track record or historical prices that can be used as the quantitative basis for choosing. The qualitative approach, on the other hand, is practically the only approach available for ICOs.

Quantitative Approach

Under this approach, you'll need to get data on a particular cryptocurrency's historical prices, ideally its historical month-end prices or if it doesn't have enough month-end samples yet, weekend prices will do. The higher the number of samples, i.e., month-end price information, the better your estimate. This is because the more samples you have, the more representative it is of the actual price behavior of a cryptocurrency.

Once you have the data, compute for the monthly (if data used are month-end prices) or weekly (if weekend prices) percentage change in price. To compute for this, subtract the previous period's (month or week) ending price from the current month's ending price and divide the amount by the previous month-end price.

<u>Month-End Price - Previous Month's End Price</u>
Previous Month's End Price

After you computed the monthly or weekly percentage price changes for all samples, compute for the mean or average percentage change for that cryptocurrency. The mean is a reasonable (not perfect but reasonable) way to estimate a cryptocurrency's possible percentage change in price in the next few weeks or months. To learn the basics of computing the mean or average using your Microsoft Excel program, watch this video:

After estimating the mean, estimate the standard deviation for the computed percentage price changes. The standard deviation can help you estimate the lowest possible expected percentage price change. To learn the basics of computing standard deviation using your Microsoft Excel program, watch this video:

Add the computed standard deviation to the average percentage price change to get the maximum expected monthly price change or return on investment. Subtract the same from the mean to get the minimum expected price change or return on investment. For example, if the computed average monthly price change for Ethereum is 15% and the standard deviation is 10%, then the maximum and minimum expected monthly returns in the future for Ethereum are 25% (15% + 10%) and 5% (15% - 10%), respectively. This means that using this simple quantitative approach, you can reasonably expect Ethereum to generate a minimum of 5% monthly returns for the succeeding months.

A caveat to this approach: these are reasonable estimates and not perfect predictions.

Qualitative Approach

Under the qualitative approach, you'll use non-numerical information to get an estimate of a cryptocurrency's chances of success - or failure. When you're considering investing in cryptocurrencies that are already being traded publicly, this can work well with your quantitative analysis in terms of coming up with a relatively comprehensive or well-rounded evaluation. But if you're looking to invest in ICOs, this is the only approach you can take because there's no historical price data that you can use for a quantitative approach.

I consider evaluating qualitative information to be an art because of the subjectivity involved in it. One person can interpret qualitative information differently from another. That's why you have to dig for as much information on an ICO as you can so you can make a very informed decision on whether to invest in an ICO or not. Your primary source of information on ICOs is their white papers. We'll talk about it in more detail in the next chapter.

Choose Your Exchange

Cryptocurrency exchanges refer to websites or platforms on which you can buy and sell cryptocurrencies. Like the New York Stock Exchange and the NASDAQ where you can buy and sell shares of stocks very conveniently, cryptocurrency exchanges allow you to do the same for coins and tokens, both for those that are already being traded and for ICO coins and tokens right after the ICOs are completed and the coins and tokens are released to the investors.

Cryptocurrency exchanges play a very important role in your investing success. As mentioned earlier, it provides a very easy way to buy and sell cryptocurrencies. If you want to buy Bitcoin, just log on to an exchange and you can access so many sellers and if you're in a hurry, hit them at their minimum offer (selling) prices. Or if you're looking to cash in on the huge price jump of the coins and tokens, you bought via an ICO by selling, just do the same. But if you don't have access to an exchange or a platform, you'll have to look for people who are willing to transact a specific cryptocurrency with you at price and exact volume that you want. It's like having to look for the nearest McDonald's branch when you can just look for one online and call for delivery. And considering the digital nature of cryptocurrencies, you won't even be able to buy and sell them outside of an exchange. So that pretty much makes registering for an exchange account moot and academic.

One of the most important criterions for choosing your cryptocurrency exchange is liquidity, which is just a fancy way of saying "average daily transaction volume" both in terms of dollar amount and number of coins and tokens transacted every day. Why is this important? Exchanges with very high average daily volumes, i.e., high liquidity, improves your chances of being able to quickly buy or sell coins and tokens. That's because it means there are a lot of buyers and sellers trusting that platform, which also means it may be relatively safer than those who have low average transaction volumes. Compare the average daily volumes of exchanges and choose the one that has the highest volume.

Another criterion for choosing your exchange is the cryptocurrency you're thinking of investing in. This is because not all exchanges carry all cryptocurrencies in the same manner that the New York Stock Exchange and the NASDAQ doesn't carry shares of stocks of all corporations in the United States.

Another criterion is security. A red flag you should watch out for are reported incidences of hacking. Because cryptocurrencies are beyond the scope and reach of any government, there are no entities you can rely on for help if your cryptocurrencies get hacked. And it's also for this reason why you should really invest in a cold storage hard wallet, which I'll talk about later on.

Lastly, compare the fees and charges. Transacting in platforms doesn't come for free you know. Fees give the people behind exchanges incentives to continue running and improving them. While the fees generally charged by cryptocurrency exchanges aren't huge, even the smallest of differences among the fees of different exchanges can become huge savings especially if you plan to go down the trading route.

Chapter 6 - How To Avoid Being Scammed

As we end this book, I'd like to discuss with you a very important aspect of investing, regardless if it's cryptocurrencies or any other financial assets: scams. Scams are the scourge of the investing community because of the damage it brings to the everybody in the investing community. Investors are duped of their hard-earned money, which in the case of the school principal I mentioned earlier can be all they have in life. It also affects legit companies looking to fund their projects because many investors may shy away from them due to traumas caused by scams either to them or people they know. And lastly, scams affect the general economy because it can deter people from investing in new businesses that need funds because of fear of being scammed.

So how can you protect yourself from scammers? One way is to know the general characteristics of most scamming victims. These include:

- Ignorance of basic investment principles like the risk-return relationship and how traditional investments like bonds and stocks work;
- High dependence on others to make investment decisions;
- Being too open or too "nice" in the face of pressure and scamming tactics employed by scammers; and
- Being too speculative.

Psychological Scam Tactics

Most scammers go for virgin victims, i.e., those who haven't been scammed yet. Why? It's because scammers and magicians or illusionists rely on the ignorance of their respective audiences with regards to the subtle ways they perform their tricks. They know that once people know what they're doing, they can never be fooled again - at least not with the same trick. Therefore, the best way to inoculate yourself against scams is to know the subtle psychological tactics they employ en route to massive scam riches. Once you're aware of these tricks, you'll be able to smell scams from a mile away. Or at least you can keep yourself from being pressured into investing in scams or even in legitimate investments that you just don't like.

There were several psychological tactics that a group in the United States called FINRA discovered in a study they conducted in 2006. The study was primarily based on numerous recordings of scammers peddling their ware to unsuspecting victims. After analyzing such recordings, FINRA researchers found that the primary psychological tactic used by scammers is persuasion. Part of their very strong persuasion skills includes asking seemingly innocent but personal questions like health, political views, and career, among others. And based on the answers they're able to get from their victims, they're able to align their product pitches with the profile they're able to construct from the victims' answers. Scammers used very specific tactics to up the persuasion ante such as:

- Source Credibility: This psychological tactic's main goal is to persuade victims to invest in their scheme by making themselves appear to be very credible investment experts by making up lofty positions or credentials. For example, a scammer might say, "As a seasoned fund manager for one of the biggest fund management companies in the world, I can smell a blockbuster investment from a mile away." This approach is meant to draw the victim's confidence to him instead of the investment itself so that the victim won't notice the inconsistencies or flaws in the purported investment scheme's details. If the investment were solid in and by itself, there's no need to refer to one's credentials.

- Social Consensus: This is a tactic that's meant to make a prospective victim feel envious of other people who have supposedly jumped on the scam's bandwagon already. Statements like "Elon Musk has already poured in millions of dollars of his personal money in this investment and people from my church have already shifted most of their investments to this one. And based on their feedback, they've never been happier with their investments' performance!" Again, the goal is to draw the focus of the victim from the shady details of the investment product to the people who have supposedly benefited much from it already and to bring the battle from the logical to the emotional realm.
- Scarcity: This is a psychological tactic that aims to convince potential victims to invest through what's called as FOMO or fear of missing out. To be fair with

scammers, it's not just them who uses this strategy because legit online marketers use it too! Under this tactic, the scammer will tell a potential victim that there's a very limited window of opportunity to get on the bandwagon and if they don't get in now, there'll be no more chances of doing so in the future. Again, this attempts to draw attention away from the investment product itself and to the feeling not being left behind, i.e., from the mental to the emotional realm.

- Reciprocity: This psychological tactic is one where scammers promise to scratch your back if you scratch theirs by investing in their scheme. For example, he or she will promise to give you up to 80% of his or her commission from the victim's investment transaction. Again, this is an attempt to draw the potential victim's attention and focus away from the logical to the emotional, which is a very bad place to be when making serious financial decisions.

- Phantom Riches: This tactic isn't just used by scammers but even by many Internet marketers who are peddling legit income-generating products. This tactic uses exaggerated statements that appeal to people's greed, which are exacerbated by ignorance of basic financial principles such as "Never has making $1,000 daily been so easy - even for newbies!" or "By investing in our product, you can triple your money in 6 to 9 months!" Again, this is an attempt to bring the battle from the realm of logic to the realm of the emotions, where many wrong financial decisions are likely to happen.

The key here is to ask a lot of questions about the investment product itself and be on the lookout for any signs of inconsistency in the details about the investment. If the person soliciting your investment seems to be changing the topic and isn't trying to avoid answering your questions by directing your focus to emotional answers instead of logical ones, chances are you're being scammed.

Scammer Alert

In the previous section, we talked about investment scam red flags that you need to watch out for from people who are soliciting investments from you. In this section, we'll look at red flags from the investment schemes themselves, i.e., highly suspicious features of the cryptocurrency investment being offered to you.

Guaranteed Returns

One of the most obvious characteristics of a cryptocurrency scam is guaranteed returns. Why is this so? To get a much better understanding of this, allow me to explain the different kinds of investments according to income, to which kind cryptocurrencies belong to, and why guaranteed returns are a big red flag that screams "I am a scam!"

Investments can be classified as either fixed or variable income. Fixed income investments are those with fixed and guaranteed income. These include bank deposits (fixed interest payments), bonds (fixed coupon payments), and property rentals (rental income). Variable income investments - as the name suggests - refer to investments whose income is neither guaranteed nor fixed. These include stocks (both price appreciation and dividends are neither guaranteed), foreign exchange or forex (price appreciations or depreciations are neither guaranteed nor fixed), and cryptocurrencies (price appreciations are neither guaranteed nor fixed and does not pay interest or dividends to its holders). And because cryptocurrencies are not fixed income or debt securities, they do not provide guaranteed income. That's why the moment someone claims that their initial coin offering or already public coins or tokens will provide a guaranteed income, that's already your cue to make run for the hills!

An even more obvious characteristic of a scam investment product is income or return that's not just guaranteed but are also very high! If you remember the risk-return principle, it says that there's a positive correlation between risk and return, i.e., the higher the expected return, the higher the risk or volatility and vice versa. A guaranteed rate of return implies a very low or non-existent risk and based on the risk-return relationship, there's no way that a low-risk security or investment can provide high returns. So whether it's a cryptocurrency trading platform such as tradecoinclub.com or an ICO, guaranteed high returns or refusal to acknowledge the possibility of loss is a glaring indicator of a cryptocurrency scam.

Very Complicated Schemes

Having enough experience with legitimate investments, I can tell you that the best and legitimate ones are those that aren't very complicated. An investment product or scheme that has so many complicated features that don't make sense even for seasoned investment veterans is a sure sign of a scam. And that's what I found with my favorite cryptocurrency scam, tradecoinclub.com.

My "upline" only laid the smack down on me regarding the full terms and conditions of tradecoinclub.com after deciding to sign up. That was when I started doubting the platform even more. His own upline - it had to take the higher ups to explain the scheme because it was so complicated that my upline himself couldn't explain it because he also doesn't understand it. He laid down so many fees and complicated but necessary withdrawal cycles that I started to smell something funny. The last straw for me was when he said that - despite not being able to fully convince me that he wasn't guaranteeing a very, very high rate of return on my investments - tradecoinclub.com would take possession of all my Bitcoins at the end of the investment period. When I asked why the platform would do that, he said it's because by then, tradecoinclub would've more than doubled my original Bitcoin investments already. By saying that, he practically admitted that tradecoinclub is guaranteeing the very high returns on my Bitcoin investments on the platform.

And what legit investment would take your principal investment away from you, right?

So if you can't wrap your head around a particular cryptocurrency, platform, or ICO especially if you've already been around the investment block, don't invest in it. Very complicated schemes are meant to dupe you into parting with your hard-earned investment money.

No Registration

If the cryptocurrency, platform, or ICO coin or token being offered to you isn't registered on any of the world's biggest and most reputable cryptocurrency exchanges, it's an obvious sign that it's a scam. It's because if the people behind it actually have plans that are at least beyond the initial offering, it would provide investors with a platform on which to actively buy and sell. By not registering with a legit exchange, they're practically saying we have no plans of helping you make sure you can sell your cryptocurrencies or buy more of them in the future.

Another registration you should look for can be found - or not found - on the cryptocurrency or investment scheme's website URL. It should be registered to have an SSL certificate, which stands for Secure Sockets Layer. An SSL-certified website has the prefix "https" at the start of its URL, i.e., https://facebook.com. Without the https prefix, it means the website didn't sign up for increased protection from hackers and as such, has a very high probability that it's either a scam or can be hacked.

Chapter 7 - How To Choose ICOs Wisely

Choosing cryptocurrencies that are already being traded publicly is a lot easier compared to choosing ICOs. For one, they already have some sort of track record to go by such as historical prices and trading volumes. For another, the solid ones are already being accepted as an alternative way of payment. ICO coins and tokens have neither and as such, information upon which to base decisions are limited.

But it doesn't mean there's no information available to make relatively well-informed decisions. It just means there are fewer information sources and you'll have to dig a bit deeper. In this final chapter, we'll talk about what information you'll need to choose ICOs wisely and indirectly, about the characteristics of great ICOs.

The White Paper

This will be your primary source of information for evaluating ICOs. Those without a white paper are highly likely to be legitimate ones in the same manner that stocks being sold through an IPO without a prospectus is a highly suspect one. White papers contain important information on the project for which the ICO is being conducted for such as what the project is, the project's purpose, the people behind the project, etc. White papers are written by different people from PR experts to lawyers and to people who are adept with both technology and business. Many white papers, such as those that emanate from countries like Singapore include disclaimers that say something like:

> *"This document should not be construed as a collective investment scheme or offer of securities. This document requires neither registration with nor approval of the Monetary Authority*

of Singapore. Investors are strongly encouraged to very carefully read this document in full and in the process of doing so, conduct due diligence."

Why are disclaimers like these necessary for white papers? It's because coins and tokens offered via ICOs are by nature investment vehicles or securities based on the Howey Test, and are therefore subject to the laws regulating financial securities in the countries wherein they're offered or originate from. By indicating such in the white papers, proponents behind ICOs are able to give the investing public a heads up about its risk and enable them to make informed decisions about the ICO. Initial coin offerings that don't have white papers are indicators of a management team or organization with neither a clear vision of the project nor a sense of accountability to the people who can help fund their projects.

A good white paper should include the following information, the quality of which may determine an ICO's success - or failure:

- The project's vision;
- The project's underlying technology;
- The specific problem in the market place that the project aims to solve or address;
- Why the problem needs to be solved or addressed;
- The solution or solutions that the project will provide that will solve the problem;
- How the coins or tokens will be shared among the investors, the core team, and the bounty;
- Timelines of important milestones that need to be achieved for the successful completion of the project concerned; and
- The people behind the project, including their respective track records.

For speculators, the white paper doesn't matter much because they're just there to speculate and make a quick buck, so the finer details don't make sense to evaluate. But for people who are planning to be long-term or buy-and-hold investors, these details matter much.

Characteristics Of Legitimate And Potentially Successful ICOs

Considering that the white paper is the primary way to evaluate the chances of success for an ICO and its corresponding token or coin, it's also a good way to sift the legitimate ones from the scams. The following are the project's vision, the team behind the project, language and focus of the paper, and information on coin supply if any.

Vision

This section provides information about what the project seeks to accomplish. It does so by enunciating on the market problem that the project wants to solve, how serious the problem is, why the problem needs to be solved, the underlying method or technology that the project will use to solve the problem, how the project will be able to solve the problem in a unique way, and if this project has the advantage of being the first mover or pioneer. The more detailed and consistent the information in this section are, the more it indicates that the project has been well thought of and planned. The graver the problem the project is trying to solve and the more unique the solution that the project will provide for addressing the problem is, the higher its chances of the ICO successfully raising enough funds to complete the project and make the tokens or coins issued truly valuable.

The Core Team

No business, organization, or project will get off the ground successfully - and stay up - without very competent and trustworthy people behind them. That's why aside from the project's vision, it's crucial that you're able to get to know the people behind the project.

So what should you look for in this section of a project's white paper? For one, you need not evaluate everybody in the team from the Head to the lowest ranking peon, I mean, staff. You just need to look at the people in the most important leadership positions such as CEO, Chairman, Chief Technology Officer, Advisory Board, and the project's development team. These are the positions that are responsible for a project's overall success. So how do you evaluate the people listed in white papers as integral parts of the organization and the development team?

The first thing you should do is make sure that the core or development team and the advisory board of the project actually has names and doesn't just feature anonymous characters. If there is no information as to the identities of these key people, consider it a legitimate scam. Only people who have something to hide will not make their identities known. I mean come on - asking investors for money without disclosure of identities? Smells a lot like a scam. And even if they have names, triple check their background online.

Assuming that they're real people, next thing you'll need to check are their credentials, i.e., educational backgrounds, work experiences, accomplishments, and scandals or issues they've been involved with if any. And to the extent possible, check out these people's relevant experiences with cryptocurrencies, blockchains, and the like. The point of doing this is to get a reasonable impression of whether or not the people behind the project have what it takes to successfully carry out the project for which funds are being solicited.

Lastly, check out if these people have Twitter, GitHub, or LinkedIn accounts featured on the official ICO website. Having such publicly accessible accounts can provide an added layer of security knowing that they're out in the open and aren't hiding their identities. Just make sure that such accounts are legit, which isn't that hard to do.

The Focus And Language Of The Paper

How a white paper is written can also give you an indirect way of evaluating whether or not an ICO will most probably succeed and whether or not it's legit. The language and focus of the paper can tell you something about the project team's capabilities as well as their possible "intentions." How?

Let's talk about focus first. Is the white paper putting too much premium on the upside of the project or the coin/token being sold via the ICO, i.e., exaggerated claims of richness and grandeur with little or no discussion on potential downsides? That may indicate a desperate attempt to raise funds to the point that the project team behind the ICO and white paper would rather not talk about the potential downsides of the project and maybe - just maybe - the downside is so huge that they're scared that when investors find out, they may not be able to raise enough funds from the ICO. Worse, it may be a scam because one of the most glaring red flags of a scam is refusal to disclose potential downsides to the point that returns seem to be practically guaranteed!

Another thing about a white paper's focus that you should look out for is the emotion it may seem to be generating from you. A white paper that feels like it's trying to make you feel overly excited and positive about it - again, to the exclusion of any sobering information like potential downsides - may indicate that the project team's trying too hard for one reason or another. Emotions are a normal part of any purchase or investment decision, but if the focus is on making you more emotional than rational, it may indicate a low-quality project that the team is desperately trying to sell or worse, a scam.

Now let's talk about language. If a white paper's written so poorly as if it were written by a preschooler, think twice about the capabilities of the people making up the project's development and management teams. A very good analogy for this are movies and TV shows about lawyers or trials. The really good movies' scriptwriters consulted with real lawyers and paralegals to make sure that the script - especially for courtroom scenes - uses terms and phrases that are actually used in the legal profession to give the movie a great semblance of reality and integrity. Can you imagine a courtroom scene where one lawyer objects to the other lawyer's tactics by saying "Your honor, I do not agree with him!" instead of "Objection, Your Honor!" In the same vein, can you imagine a white paper using amateur language or a tone that's unprofessional? What impression does that give you about the people behind the project? Right!

Token Rewards
More and more newer coins and tokens have evolved by adding a new feature by which investors can earn income. Two of these innovations include master nodes and staking. How can investors possibly earn income through these?

Master nodes refer to a server on a blockchain network that is used for specialized functions that ordinary nodes in a network can't such as private transactions and direct send or instant transactions. If an ICO features coins or tokens that have or will add master nodes in the near future, it means it will allow users to host master nodes for that network and in the process, allow them to earn passive income by simply holding on to their tokens or coins. This feature has very good chances of higher price increase and as such, can give you potentially higher returns on your investment compared to ICOs with no master nodes for their tokens or coins.

If you want to earn more income or extra units of coins or tokens, you can host a master node and get paid. But for this, you'll need to have good programming skills, particularly Linux, and a sizeable amount of coin or token holdings. Hosting a master node isn't for the technically illiterate and people with small token or coin holdings.

Staking refers to receiving coin or token rewards in exchange for holding a specific amount of coins for a specific period of time as a way of supporting the coin or token's network. It's like a bank deposit where your account is paid interest for keeping your money in the bank. As with bank deposits, the factors that will affect the amount of staking rewards you may receive are the length of time you'll stake your tokens or coins and the interest rate. Staking is exclusive to proof-of-stake (PoS) networks only and will prevent you from selling the coins for the period of time you committed to holding it. ICOs that feature staking in their coins or tokens may provide you with a higher return than ICOs that don't because of this passive income feature.

Coin Or Token Supply

The number of coins or tokens that will be issued can have a direct impact on the success of an ICO as well as your chances of earning a very high return on your investment. Why? The law of supply and demand, which states that if supply is less than demand, the price of that good will be higher. Therefore, ICOs with lower supplies of coins or tokens have a pretty good chance of generating superior returns for its investors compared to ICOs with a supply level.

To give you a better idea of how high your returns (and consequently, your risks) can be vis-a-vis an ICOs coins supply, here are some estimates of risk and rewards according to coin supply:

- Over 1 billion tokens = low returns and risk;
- Between 100 million to 1 billion tokens = medium returns and risk, which is the sweet spot;
- Between 10 million to 100 million tokens = higher returns and risk; and
- Less than 10 million tokens = very high returns and very high risk.

Online Presence
The more visible an ICO and its company is on the Internet particularly social media, the higher its chances of success, which makes it highly likely that you'll earn very high returns on your ICO investment. But what does online presence

on Facebook, Twitter, YouTube, and forums like Reddit and Bitcoin Talk have to do with an ICOs success? A couple of things.

For one, more visibility can project a greater sense of integrity, accountability, and reputation. Being out in the open where investors can easily interact with and ICO's company can be construed as confidence in the project's success and that the company has nothing to hide, both of which can help make investors feel safer with the thought of investing in that ICO. The more confidence the investing public has in an ICO, the higher the chances of it generating much needed funds for its project and very handsome returns for its investors.

As mentioned earlier, having legit profiles on LinkedIn and Twitter that are posted on the company's webpage are very good ways to know more about the people running the project and whether or not they're very capable of carrying out the task. Having an active and engaging Facebook and Twitter accounts can make it easier for investors to ask questions and get answers relatively quickly. And being active on forums may indicate substantial interest in the ICO, which increases its odds of success.

Cryptocurrency Glossary

#

51% Attack – when at least 51% of the network's computing power is controlled by a single person or group, they may carry out harmful transactions with malicious intent.

A-B

Address – An identifier made up of a string of random characters that allows blockchain transactions to happen between individuals or entities. Usually accompanied by a private key for accessing funds

Altcoin – Cryptocurrencies or tokens other than Bitcoin

Arbitrage – Taking full advantage of a price difference on one currency between two exchanges; usually mentioned in the context of the ETH price on US and Korean exchanges

ASIC – Acronym for Application Specific Integrated Circuit, these are made ONLY for mining and are cheaper in power cost than a standard mining rig. Can use Wi-Fi or Ethernet to connect to a network or computer

ATH - All-Time-High. The highest ever-price point of a cryptocurrency.

Bagholder – A person who is holding on to an Altcoin after a crash caused by a pump-and-dump scheme. May also refer to a person who is hanging on to a crypto coin whose value is dropping and has no real prospect for the future

Bearish – Commonly termed a Bear market in stocks, when the price is widely expected to fall

Bit – Commonly used to describe a sub-unit of the Bitcoin. 1 Bitcoin is equal to 1000 bits

Bitcoin – The very first open-source and decentralized cryptocurrency

Bitcoin Cash (BCH) – Created in 2017, BCH is a copy of Bitcoin blockchain with a higher block size (8MB as opposed to Bitcoin's 1MB); created after a fork

Block – A data record on the blockchain, more like a ledger page and containing details of transactions that are pending. Every 10 minutes or so, each block will be confirmed and added to the blockchain by miners

Block Explorer – A tool found online that lets you look through all Blockchain transactions and provides information such as the hash rate of the network

Block Height – How many blocks are connected on the blockchain

Block Reward - A reward or incentive to miners who can correctly calculate a block hash when mining. When transactions are verified, new coins get generated and the miner is given a percentage of these as his reward

Blockchain – The shared or distributed ledger where all cryptocurrency transactions get stored. Each block is affixed the next, creating a tamper-proof record of every single transaction ever made in a chain of blocks

Breakout – The point at which the market price of a digital asset or crypto coin goes past a resistance or support level that has already been defined

BTC – The official acronym for Bitcoin

Bullish – Described as a Bull market in stocks, this is when the price is widely expected to rise

Buy Wall – A buy order that is massive, stopping the market price from dropping until the buy order has been fully completed

Buying Pressure – This happens when a high percentage of traders are purchasing, an indicator that they are expecting an increase in market price

C-D

Central Ledger – A ledger that is being maintained by a centralized agency

Circulating Supply – The total number of a specific coin in circulation at any one time, and available for trading or spending

Cold Storage – A safer way of storing your cryptocurrency offline, stopping it from being lost through hacking. There are several ways of doing this but the most common include:

- Print a supplied QR code for a software wallet and keep it safe
- Take the files from the software wallet and store them on an external storage source, storing that away safe
- Use of a hardware wallet

Commodity Money – A currency whose value is a result of the commodity it is derived from

Confirmation – Successful hash of a transaction that is then added to the blockchain

Consensus – When all the network participants are in total agreement on transaction validity; this means that every copy of the blockchain is identical

Cryptocurrency – A digital currency produced by solving mathematical algorithms; decentralized and secured with cryptography so it cannot be manipulated or counterfeited.

Cryptographic Hash Function – A unique hash value of fixed size is produced by a cryptographic hash form transaction inputs of various sizes. An example of this is the SHA-256 algorithm

Cryptography – Math that is used by cryptocurrency to provide security on a high level. For example, with Bitcoin, the cryptography is used to make sure that the blockchain cannot be corrupted and the contents of a wallet cannot be spent by an unauthorized person

DAO – Acronym for Decentralized Autonomous Organization. This is venture capital fund that was based on Ethereum and, famously, got hacked in 2016. This resulted in a loss of around one-third of the funds and in a hard-fork happening not long after. This is referred to as one of the biggest problems to hit Ethereum to date

DaPP – Acronym for Decentralized Applications. These are open source applications that operate without human intervention. All data is kept on a blockchain, the incentive is by way of tokens and operates on a Proof of Value protocol

DASH – A cryptocurrency created in 2014, with a basis in the Bitcoin software but much more anonymous. Its features mean that transactions can never, ever be traced to any individual. Otherwise known as DarkCoin and XCoin.

DCA – Stands for Dollar Cost Averaging and used to reduce portfolio volatility. This is done by the spreading of buys and sells over a much longer time

DDoS – Acronym for Distributed Denial of Service. An attack of this kind involves one attacker and multiple computers and is designed to drain all the resources of the initial target. Some exchanges have been the victim of this kind of attack

Decentralized – No central agency, no central function and no central power which leads to there being no single PoF – point of failure. This leads to much higher security and trust

Difficulty – The ease or otherwise of the success of mining a transaction block

Digital Signature - Generated through the public key, this is code that is attached to each electronic document as a way of verifying both the identity of the sender and the contents of the document

Distributed Consensus – An agreement made collectively by the network computers that they will work in a P2P manner that is decentralized, with no need for any central agency to stop dishonesty on the network

Distributed Ledger – These are ledgers that store data on them across a network of computers or nodes. They do not have a currency and they may be private and permissioned

Distributed Network – A network where all the data and the processing power are distributed across the network nodes instead of in one central database

Double Spending – When money is spent twice – this cannot happen with cryptocurrency because of the verification process in place for each transaction

Dump – When a large amount of cryptocurrency is sold at the current market value by an individual or a group, resulting in the market price diving

E-F

EEA – Acronym for Enterprise Ethereum Alliance, which is a group of corporations and startups, with some very big names included, all trying to work out the best way of sing Ethereum

ERC-20 – An Ethereum token standard which is in place to ensure the tokens behave predictably. Because of this, they can easily be exchanged and will work with any ERC-20 compatible decentralized application. Most ICO tokens are compliant with the ERC-20 standard.

Ether (ETH) – The currency used on Ethereum to pay for tasks and transaction fees which are based on gas price and gas limit – these fees are paid in ETH

Ethereum – A decentralized platform built on the blockchain; used to run apps that use smart contracts and with the aim of eliminating issues that surround interference by third-parties, fraud, and censorship.

Ethereum Classic (ETC) – After the much-publicized DAO attack, the Ethereum blockchain split in a hard fork that was carried out to bring back the money that was stolen. ETC carries on as the original blockchain with the support of all those who believe that the blockchain should be entirely immutable and did not support the hard fork

EVM – Acronym for Ethereum Virtual Machine (EVM), which is a Turing Complete machine that will allow EVM Byte code to be executed by anyone. All Ethereum nodes run on this to ensure consensus is maintained across the blockchain

Exchange – A platform whereby users can exchange fiat currency for digital currency and vice versa

Fiat Currency – A currency that has little to no value and is produced by governments as and when needed or when the value needs to be tempered down. They do not have the backing of any commodity but are legal tender. This is the currency that you carry in your pocket today

FinCEN – A US Treasury agency, otherwise known as the Financial Crimes Enforcement Network. It was started as a way of protecting financial systems from illegal use and as a way of fighting back against money launderers. It is also responsible for collecting financial intelligence and analyzing it. This is the main US agency for the imposition of regulations on Bitcoin trading exchanges.

Flipping – A strategy in investing where a purchase is made with the sole purpose of selling it for a quick profit. As far as ICOs are concerned, flipping is the investment of the tokens before they hit the exchanges and then selling them on when they reach the secondary market

FOMO – Acronym for Fear of Missing Out. This is a reference to an apprehensive feeling of missing an investment opportunity that has the potential to be profitable which then leads to feelings of regret later down the line

Fork – A change to the cryptocurrency protocol that is not backward compatible. Forks tend to happen when a separate version of the blockchain is created by network nodes using a different protocol version. This second blockchain is not compatible with the original blockchain software, resulting in 2 that run side by side on different sections of the network.

FUD – Acronym for Fear, Uncertainty, and Doubt. It is when negative or false information is spread about, leading to a false perception of something

FUDster – A person responsible for spreading FUD

G-H

Gas – The amount of processing power that is used for processing transactions on the Ethereum network. The amount depends on the simplicity or complexity of the transaction with Smart Contracts among the highest in cost

Gas Limit – A term that describes how much a specific user is prepared to spend on any one transaction on the Ethereum network. There must be sufficient gas to execute the transaction, including all resources needed and, if there is any gas left over, it is returned back to the user

Gas Price – The amount in Eth for each of the gas units on any one transaction. The person who starts the transaction pays the required price and there is a priority system – high price transactions are executed first.

Genesis Block – The very first verified and processed block of any new blockchain, sometimes called Block 0 or, in some cases, Block 1

Going Long – Margin trade that will profit if the price goes up

Going Short – Margin trade that profits if the price goes down

Gwei – An Ether denomination, the one that gas prices tend to be measured in the most. 10,000,000,00 gwei is equal to 1 Ether

Hard Cap – The absolute maximum that an ICO will raise; once they get to the hard cap, they will stop raising funds

Hard Fork – A fork that will make any transactions that were invalid, valid and those that were valid will be rendered invalid. A hard fork requires that every node on the network is upgraded to use the latest software

Hard Wallet – A physical device that stores your cryptocurrency offline; general seen as the best and most secure storage facility

Hash Rate – The maximum hashes that are performed by a miner in a specified period, usually 1 second

Hash – Algorithm that converts variable data into fixed data or a shorter length

HODL – A meme that originally came about as a result of a spelling error in a Bitcoin forum, HODL is also referred to as "Hold on for Dear Life" or "Buy and Hold." It refers to a strategy of making a long-term investment irrespective of how volatile the market is.

Hybrid PoS/PoW -A consensus algorithm that uses the Proof of Stake and Proof of Work. This provides for a better balance between the voters and the miners and creates a system whereby the community is governed by both insiders and outsiders.

I-K

ICO – An Initial Coin Offering, much like the IPO or Initial Public Offering seen in stocks and shares. ICOs are set up to raise the required amount of money for a new project in cryptocurrency by offering a specific number of the coins for the public to buy. These coins are set at a base price and, over the long term, that price will go up or down depending on supply and demand.

IOTA (MIOTA) – A cryptocurrency and a distributed open source ledger that appeared in 2015, that is NOT based on the blockchain. Instead, it uses Tangle, a brand-new type of ledger. Features include no feed, better scalability and more security for transactions and it is almost entirely focused on IoT or the Internet of Things.

KYC – Acronym for Know Your Client and is also used to Know Your Customer. The guidelines for KYC state that all potential clients to any financial institution must be checked to make sure that they are real people and can provide identity verification. This is used by most of the big cryptocurrency exchanges

L-M

Lightning Network – a P2P system, off the blockchain and low-latency that allows for cryptocurrency micropayments to be made. Features include better scalability, instant payment, cheaper cost transactions and works cross-chan. There is no need for anyone to make a public transaction on the blockchain and smart contracts are used for enforcing the security of each transaction

Limit Order / Limit Buy / Limit Sell – These are orders that traders place for buying and selling when the price of a cryptocurrency gets to a specific point. They are much like the 'For Sale' signs that you see outside a house and are usually used in conjunction with Market Orders.

Liquidity – Describes the purchase and/or sale of a digital asset together with the process of the price staying consistent between each transaction

Litecoin (LTC) – Another cryptocurrency, created in 2011, by Charlie Lee who used to work for Google. Features include SegWit and use of the Lightning Network for low-cost faster processing times.

Margin Trading – Risking the crypto coins that you own to intensify your trades – this is NOT recommended for beginners, only for those who are very experienced in trading. It should also not be done on all exchanges, only certain ones

Market Cap – A cryptocurrency's total value, calculated through the multiplication of the total coin supply by the current market price of one unit

Market Capitalization – Total value of the supply in circulation of any give cryptocurrency

Market Order / Market Buy / Market Sell – Basic sale or purchase of a cryptocurrency at the current market price on an exchange. The market buy purchases the cryptocurrency at the cheapest available price and the market sell will sell at the highest available price

mBTC – A Bitcoin denomination worth about 0.001 BTC or one-thousandth of one bitcoin

MEW – Acronym for MyEtherWallet, a free online site for the generation of software wallets

Mining – The process of verifying transactions before putting them on the blockchain and is also how new coins are produced. Anyone with the right hardware and internet access can mine for cryptocurrency but the costs of power and the hardware, usually required on an industrial scale, will limit who can do it, specifically with Bitcoin

Mining Farm – A warehouse or large room loaded with mining rigs for multiple processing of the blockchain algorithms

Mining Pool – a group of miners who pool their computing and pricing power to mine. The payouts are lower but easier to get

Mining Rig - A specifically designed computer set up for mining, containing many top of the range GPUs for the maximum amount of processing power. Very expensive to purchase, these are usually out of the range of Joe Public and usually used by mining farms

Monero (XMR) – A cryptocurrency that came about in 2014, with a focus almost entirely on being scalable and private. It will run on multiple platforms, including Linux, Mac, and Windows, as well as Android. Transactions are not traceable to any specific person or true identity

Multisig – The official term for addresses that require multiple users to use public keys to seed a blockchain address. These are much more secure and less likely to be hacked into

N-O

NEM (XEM) – Reference to a cryptocurrency and a management platform for a range of assets, such as records of ownership, currency, supply chains, and so on Extra features includes multi-sig, message encryption and much more

NEO – A cryptocurrency that appeared in 2014 and is also the name of the first blockchain (open source) in China. Much like Ethereum, NEO facilitates smart contracts and DaPPs but suffers from issues with compatibility of coding languages.

Node - A computer on the blockchain network that holds and maintains a copy of the blockchain

Oracles – These provide smart contracts with data, bridging the gap between the blockchain and the real world.

P-Q

P2P– Acronym and common terms for Peer to Peer. This technology has long been used on the net for downloading and uploading files. In terms of cryptocurrency, it is referring to the decentralized transactions that take place between two or more parties without the interference of any third-party or regulatory body

Paper Wallet – Hard copy of your wallet with relevant information, including addresses and keys. Often used as a more secure way of storing cryptocurrency without using software solutions

Pre-Sale – A coin sale that happens before an ICO goes for public participation

Private Key – A random data string that provides access to the contents of a particular wallet. Much like a password, they must be kept safe because the loss of or theft of the key means losing access to your wallet forever.

Proof of Stake (PoS) – One of the blockchain algorithms, provides rewards for the solving of difficult puzzles or mathematical problems so that a distributed consensus may be achieved. Different to the PoW, transactions can be validated, and new blocks may be created based on the stake of an individual, such as the total number of coins that they own. Also uses less power than PoW.

Proof of Work (PoW) – Another blockchain algorithm that gives the reward to the person who solves the problem first. Miners are in competition with one another to solve mathematical problems so that the next block can be added to the chain. Because the service requester requires service time, cyber-attacks and spam attacks can be prevented.

PSP – Acronym for Payment Service Provider. These are agents for those places that will accept payments online

Public Address – The hash of the public key or blockchain address; they act the same way as an email address does, and can be made known publicly, unlike the private key.

Public Key – A string of alphanumeric characters that take on the job of a blockchain address when private keys are hashed with them for digital signing of any transaction. This key may be given to other individuals for the purpose of sending and receiving cryptocurrency

Pump – When an individual or group buys a lot of one type of coin at the current market price, pushing up the price

Pump and Dump Scheme – A scheme by which a project that doesn't have any real basis is hyped up to push up the price; the purchasers then sell as soon as the launch is made to make a tidy profit, thus potentially pushing the price back down again

QR code – Acronym for Quick Response code. A 2D image in a block that can be scanned on any device with a code reader (smartphone, tablet, etc.). The block image contains data and is sometimes used for bitcoin address ending. You will find one of these when you transfer your wallet offline.

R-S

Raiden Network – An Ethereum protocol change due to being implemented soon. This will also for transfers to be made at high speed, much like the Lightning Network from Bitcoin

Resistance Level – A point at which the price of a commodity or asset resists any more increases because of conditions in the market

Ripple (XRP) – A cryptocurrency that was based on OpenCoin and also the name of the payment platform (open source) where the currency may be transferred between users. The aim of Ripple is to enable a global payment system in real-time

ROI – Acronym for Return on Investment and refers to the percentage of profit made compared to the investment initially made. For example, 100% ROI would indicate that the investor has made 100% of their investment, doubling their money

Satoshi Nakamoto – The founder of Bitcoin, an unknown person or group of persons responsible for the Bitcoin protocol

Satoshi – A subunit of a bitcoin, 0.00000001 BTC is equal to 1 BTC

Scrypt – A cryptographic algorithm in use by Litecoin, much quicker than SHA-256 and uses less processing time and power

Segregated Witness (SegWit) – A process that increases the limit in a blockchain block size by moving the data for digital signatures to the end of each transaction to provide more capacity. Each transaction is split into two – the data and the signature

Sell Wall – A Massive sell order that stops the market price from increasing until the whole order has been completed

Selling Pressure – This happens when a high percentage of traders sell, an indication that they believe the price is going to drop

SEPA – Acronym for Single European Payment Area. This was set up as an EU integration payment system to facilitate payments in Euros between nations

SHA-256 – A cryptographic algorithm in use by some cryptocurrencies. Unlike Scrypt, Sha-256 uses more processing power and takes more time, thus making it more profitable for miners to form pools rather than attempting to mine alone

Sharding – A method by which network nodes can hold a part-copy of a blockchain instead the entire blockchain. This increases speed and performance

Shill – An individual who hypes up a cryptocurrency, over and above what it really is, because it is likely to be a scam

Smart Contracts – Usually run on the Ethereum platform, although others are now appearing, a Smart Contract is an automated system where two parties or more place their digital assets into a contract for later distribution. The contract will run without any downtime because it is automated, and it will only be completed when a specified event is triggered. An example would be Part A agreeing to pay Party B 100 BTC on receipt of an electronic key for a car hire agreement. The 100 BTC are placed into escrow and are only released on receipt of the key or if both the key and the BTC are placed into escrow at the same time, both will be released on a preset date.

Soft Cap – The absolute minimum that an ICO is looking to raise. If they do not reach that amount, the ICO will be canceled and any funds raised will be sent back to those who provided them

Soft Fork – Different from a hard fork, soft forks mean that transactions that were valid before the fork are invalid, the old network nodes will treat the new blocks ad being valid and, as such, the soft fork is backward compatible. Most network miners will need to upgrade to the new software for enforcement

Soft Wallet – Wallet software that stores cryptocurrencies online, on mobile devices or on computers

Solidity – The programming language used by Ethereum for smart contracts

Stable Coin – Cryptocurrency that has very low volatility and can be used for trading against the whole market

Support Level – A point at which market conditions stop decreases in price

T-V

TA – Acronym for Technical Analysis or Trend Analysis. This references the process by which current market charts are examined to try to predict whether the market is going to go up or down

Testnet – A blockchain developed for testing purposes so that they do not waste assets on the primary blockchain

The Flippening – Expected to happen in the future, when the market cap for Ethereum goes past that of Bitcoin, which would make Ethereum the single most valuable cryptocurrency of all time.

Token – What allows for decentralized and open source networks to be created and also incentives for people to take part in the network. Tokens have been made more popular through Ethereum and now there are many token networks in existence

Total Supply – The total amount of tokens or coins that exist for a specified digital asset. This includes those already in circulation as well as any that have been reserved or locked onto the network

Trading Volume – The total traded cryptocurrency during a specified time period

Transaction Block – A group of transactions that have been certified and pulled into a block. These transactions are then hashed, and the block added to the end of the blockchain

Transaction Fee – Every transaction carried out with cryptocurrency attracts a small fee. The miner for each block receive a percentage of the total block fees as their reward

Turing Complete – A machine that is capable of computing anything that needs to be computed. If any other programmable machine can compute it, the Turing Complete machine can also compute it. The EVM is an example of this.

Vitalik Buterin - One of the founders of the Ethereum network and the most well-known one.

Volatility – This refers to the movements of the price of a currency, recorded over a set period of time, A high volatility means that the price is unstable and, although it may rise fast, it can also crash hard without warning

W-Z

Wallet – A software or hardware solution for the storage of private cryptographic keys. These include software clients that let a user view their transactions and create new ones on the blockchain that the wallet is meant for. Most wallets are tied to being used on one blockchain only, for example, Bitcoin or Ethereum.

Wei – The smallest known Ether denomination, 1000000000000000000 Wei is equal to 1 Ether

Whale –An individual or group who own sufficient capital to conduct massive orders that may be used for market manipulation

Whitelist- A list of participants who have been approved and registered to take part in an ICO or in a Pre-Sale

Whitepaper – A document that is released prior to a project. The best known is the Bitcoin whitepaper that was released the year before Bitcoin and explained what it was all about and what its objectives were

Wire Transfer – A method of sending funds electronically from one person to another, often used as a way of getting fiat currency back from an exchange

Zerocoin – A new project with the goal of introducing real anonymity to Bitcoin network.

Zero Confirmation Transaction – A transaction made on the Bitcoin network that has been sent out to the nodes but is awaiting processing into a block Sometimes termed as unconfirmed transactions

Conclusion

Thanks for buying this book. I hope that you have learned much from it. But more importantly, I hope that through this book, I was able to inspire you to act whether it's to read more materials about ICOs or to go and start investing in one already. The bottom line is knowledge is only potential power and its true power lies in the application or acting on it.

But I also want to caution you: apply or act upon one or two learnings at a time. Why? Applying everything at once can be both overwhelming and dangerous. Overwhelming because ICO investing - especially evaluating which ones to invest in - isn't a piece of cake considering the relatively technical nature of the financial assets involved. Dangerous because applying everything at once runs you the risk of not being thorough in your evaluations and decisions, which can increase your risks for missteps. So while I encourage acting immediately, I recommend performing such actions with great care.

Here's to your success my friend! Cheers!

About the Author

Jack Monroe is a Cryptocurrency specialist, Entrepreneur and Author of numerous books to help others with growth and development. As an early Entrepreneur, his focus has switched towards Cryptocurrency investment. Trading, Mining and investing in Bitcoin, Ethereum, Litecoin, Ripple, Ethos, and other Altcoins has given Jack a future and the knowledge to provide valuable skills and training to others in the world of Cryptocurrency.

Jack Monroe is a family man who only aspires to build a strong foundation for his family. He believes that with hard work and mindfulness, success and abundance will come. With his accomplishments, Jack chose to help others understand that Successful Investing is about managing risk, not avoiding it.

Initial Coin Offering

www.ingramcontent.com/pod-product-compliance
Lightning Source LLC
Chambersburg PA
CBHW052322220526
45472CB00001B/221